Evenlode

Charles Bennett

Oversteps Books

First published in 2013 by

Oversteps Books Ltd
6 Halwell House
South Pool
Nr Kingsbridge
Devon
TQ7 2RX
UK

www.overstepsbooks.com

ISBN 978-1-906856-39-7

Printed in Great Britain by imprint digital, Devon

Acknowledgements

Grateful thanks are due to the editors of the following publications where these poems, sometimes in earlier versions, first appeared: *10th Muse, Borderlines, The Coffeehouse, Cornwall Advanced Motorists News, Countryside Tales, The Dark Horse, Dreamcatcher, The Edinburgh Review, Envoi, Iota, Magma, Other Poetry, The Oxford Magazine, Poetry London, Poetry in the Waiting Room, Raindog, The Red Wheelbarrow, The SHOp, Stand, Staple.*

A Note on the Herbal Poems

Information concerning the individual properties of these herbs may be found by consulting Gerard's *Herbal* (the 'old herbal Gerard' of Edward Thomas's 'Lob'), or by referring to *A Modern Herbal* by Mrs M. Grieve.

In 'Sanicle', the story of Gwydion and Llew is taken from the Fourth Branch of *The Mabinogion*. 'Horehound' imagines an encounter with my great-grandfather, the herbalist John Bennett.

The extracts that appear as epigraphs to the Sweeney poems are taken from J G O'Keeffe's 1913 translation.

This book is for Alan Byford – who likes the names

These names
Purify a corner of my mind

On Reading a Book on Common Wild Flowers
Patrick Kavanagh

Naming these things is the love-act and its pledge;
For we must record love's mystery without claptrap,
Snatch out of time the passionate transitory.

'The Hospital' Patrick Kavanagh

[...] the names
Half-decorate, half-perplex, the thing it is:
At least, what that is clings not to the names
In spite of time. And yet I like the names.

'Old Man', or 'Lad's Love'
Edward Thomas

SELFHEAL

I've spent all winter writing about wild flowers
pressing their names like seeds between the pages.

By the time I come up for air in late summer
these lines will be overgrown and I shall be cured.

Contents

Herb Bennet

song with yellow notes
put out by frost

comma to grip your dress
whenever you swish

glimmer of petal-confetti
dripped on gravel

star to unspeak the venom
of a stepped-on snake

leaf to splint and knit
the green snap

prayer in the slather of rain
for better weather

root to cleave a seam
through soft sleep

wash to tickle the speck
of spilt freckles

salve to ease the bruise
when you ups-a-daisy

fuzzle of awns that follow
you back in the house

scent of a name spoken
when the buds open

Coram's Fields

10am

A man with a dozen yellow tulips
is reading the notice board on Emerald Passage:
Mila Campnoy from the Calthorpe Institute
will talk about *Flowers & Their Uses*.

He thinks about going and meanwhile
the yellow of his February tulips
is making the man at Bikefix sing
a small repairing song.

11am

At Kennard's Good Food this morning
they're stacking the shelves with honey,
jars of Tasmanian Leatherwood
and Active Manuka –

and a large delirious bee
has dived into acres of snowdrops
on the pavement outside Dawson Flowers
like his own private miracle.

12 noon

The cat who's fast asleep
in the window of Matchless Prints
twitches his ears whenever
they open a tin of tuna

at Rita's Sandwich Bar across the street,
where two white slices side by side
are freshly opened pages
in the book of Tuesday.

1pm

When a man on his way to lunch
stops on the corner of Great Ormond
and waves 'after you' at a car,
the driver flashes her lights

and waves 'after you' at him.
So they laugh at each other and smile
keeping the space between them wide open
in a long, slow moment of giving way.

2pm

On the corner of Mecklenburg & Heathcote
a woman is calling a name to an open window.
In one long easy breath she floats it up
like an arrow at the top of its flight.

Trees in St George's Gardens
are all of a tremble
and everyone comes to their window
except for the person she's calling.

3pm

Over a pint at The Duke
the man who once posted a paper dart
through the letterbox of the Brazilian
Aeronautical Commission in Europe,

and famously showed the Egypt Exploration Society
how Wilson, Kepple & Betty used to dance,
is teaching the lunchtime barmaid how to land
a skittish Fairey Seafox on the Nile.

4pm

From the window of Griffith & Partners
The Grammar of Japanese Language
has opened the wings of its cover
and flown like an origami blackbird

to the branches of bonsai trees
in Brownlow Mews. Each evening
it sings haiku from the leafy pages
written by Tatui Baba in 1904.

5pm

In a space between the song of three robins
on a bench in Saint George's Gardens
I'm waiting for you to arrive. Whatever
it is that's delayed you, I don't mind –

I'm happy to watch a small gap in the clouds
opening wider and wider. I can sit here quietly
by the Thomas Falconer Obelisk
for as long as it takes.

At Mena Martin's Guesthouse

Tonight I'm washing my face in this porcelain basin
where both the taps are crowned with a letter *C*.

On my left is the chill of a scamper through icy water
as skylarks spilled your name at Carrigskeewaun.

To the right I'm cast adrift on a single mattress
with toes that search for you and find the wall.

Tomorrow I'll bring you the present of not being absent
and the cold and also the cold I found in Ireland.

Porthgwarra

Sit with me here at Porthgwarra
let's listen to the bell in the buoy

and notice the way whatever we hadn't noticed
is coming to rest in a greeny-blue interval

between the strike of one sour sea-note and the next.
And even if it's true that the voice in the buoy

is the cry of a drowning man,
after a while the sun will warm these stones

and the day swing round by itself
on the right heading. So let's sit quietly here

as everything settles into place –
and then when we speak, let's speak

at the same time and state the obvious:
This is the life we'll say – and yes, it will be.

At Whitesands Bay

A battered Peugeot dawdles down the car park
then rolls to a stop so its driver can look at the sea.
When she opens the door her terrier dog scuttles out
and takes himself off for a widdle and a scamper by the surf
while she remains behind with the *Western Telegraph* –
each of them pleasing the other by suiting themselves
then sharing the biscuits in the glove-box.

And if some days you wanted to be the dog,
or else when the mood was on you maybe the driver –
I wouldn't mind so long as when I came back
and leapt with a yelp by your window
you'd open the door a fraction to let me in,
and after we'd had a biscuit (or possibly two)
whoever wasn't the dog would drive home.

Salthouse

When we walked up the hill above Salthouse
and saw, looking down where we'd been,

ourselves on the beach waving –
we were here and there and no-place,

coming and going at once, perceiving
the speckled clouds as sleeping seals;

we dipped our toes in the breeze
and watched from the hill's shoreline

a kestrel come in with the tide
and hold his stillness open

over the ship weathervane
of a church that was floating and drowned –

his shadow on the ground beneath him
the anchor that kept him aloft.

Common Freshwater Fishes of Britain & Ireland

Perch ~ Pike ~ Roach ~ Rudd ~ Tench
I'm reading in bed with you asleep already

and as I turn each page with a leisurely *sloosh*
I notice a glimmer and dash as all manner of fish

slip from their lavishly full-colour-illustrated places
and swim with a bright shiver of dorsal and pectoral

down to the warm and shady undercurrents of our room
where a lazy Dorset chalk-stream summer breeze

is wafting the speckled pebbles that cover the floor
and the Common Freshwater Fishes of Britain & Ireland

come to be told their names and enter their nature
as I open a slithery book of green riverweed

and recite in a water-voice of fluvial English
Perch ~ Pike ~ Roach ~ Rudd ~ Tench.

Ash

I love to see the word of last night's sleep
spelt out in the wrinkles of our bed.

We shape a sound by lying back to back
and curling round our spines until they meet.

A sound like shingle, shushed by drowsy waves
or the graft of A with E in *Curriculum Vitæ.*

As if we wrote the grapheme known as Ash
and spoke a tree awake by saying our breath.

The word we make is warm in the soft dark,
smooth as hands that wander along a spine,

and snug as upturned boats drawn up the beach
above the reach of spring tides overnight.

Birds Nesting in Dunsfold Orchard

And here in the cup of your hands
is a nest for rain   for a bird
of water to open its spilt wings

Here is a space where a song
might grow like a leaf   could fly
down summer to the fruit

Winter's blossom sang itself
to sleep   and here is new-laid snow
feathering the breeze

A blackbird's eye peeps
from an apple pip   plump
dark notes to sing a tree

In the nest of your hands a day
has come to land   you can only
keep it safe by letting it go

The title is taken from the earliest recorded work by Thomas Warton, 1728-1790. Warton's poem was written when he was eight years old and is set in his grandfather's orchard.

Everdon Stubbs

Rainfall

There's a forest on the top of a hill
where the trees are singing –
their leaves are birds who chaunt

in green voices. This morning
they sound like a downpour, as if
each leaf were a drop of falling rain.

Stand in the middle of the wood
and you'll hear what they're saying:
When rain comes to sing on the hill

we are drenched with music –
will you come and walk beneath us
with the song of rain in your eye?

Storm-fall

At first the storm is just
a jostle and rush in our leaves
and when push comes to shove

our strength is in knowing
how to give. When the axe
of lightning cracks, and severs

us all asunder, we bear
the brunt of thunder
as the sky is rent by a shudder.

Come in under the canopy,
shelter beneath a holly
as we splash and thresh.

Snowfall

We're stretching to reach
this blossom as it slips
through our grasp,

but once we take hold –
how heavy the sky becomes.
No wonder it falls

like the seeds of a strange star,
ready to grow silence
wherever it lands.

What are you waiting for?
You could write the first word
on a white field.

Nightfall

At the end of light
there are voices, sobs
and sighs in the trees

as all the birds of the forest
fall asleep. Tonight they dream
the songs they'll sing

tomorrow. What you hear
in the middle of the night,
is the sound of your own music

trying to find you, the dream
of a song taking shape
while you're asleep.

Gaelic Notes in the Book of Deer

A jackdaw taps at the lid
of the fish-pond's closed eye.

Water is looking down –
carp are plump clouds in a sky of silt.

Bulbous with summer a swimmer
is a feast-hoard of days.

They always only peep at both sides
stay open even when asleep.

At dark they drown in a dream's sweet depth –
star-spawn in the night-pond.

Their weeping is the origin of water
and why the sea is salt.

Inky beneath the roof clasp
I sink to the deep of dark-sight.

The Book of Deer is a small, tenth century illuminated gospel book. It was in the possession of The Monastery of Deer (a sixth century foundation located at Old Deer in Aberdeenshire). Other than this manuscript, nothing remains of the monastery itself. In the twelfth century, the monks began to use blank spaces and margins to record both legal and legendary material written in Scots Gaelic. These 'notitiae' are the first continuous examples of the language. The poem is voiced for a scribe, and imagines a gloss in the margin.

Chough

give a gruff cough
then sniff red bills beneath the turf

as if they muttered *yes, yes, yes*
with every probe and stab of salty grass –

they crackle alight and strike their sharp call
tumbling aloft in a scatter, a floppy roll,

they collapse – lollop – plunge
like a verb the wind has spoken, a hinge

of wings that glint between the hill
and the sea's furrow. Fire crow. Fire crow. You spill

and scribble in the margins of air's psalter –
a mischievous gloss, half-otter, half-eel, you saunter

towards a spin, then fold your ragged W into a dive.
Perhaps you are telling me something by how you behave.

But now you flip and veer as if you can never have enough
of this nonsense. As you fall off the air I hear God's laugh.

Blackberries at Cwmtydu

Glossy along the bramble's straggling stem
are berries
dropped like breves on a prickly stave.

Heavy with music ripened in sweet juice
the bushes
are a dark song written by sunlight.

The Bumblebees' Nest

was a hole as round as my thumb
a secret black well which oozed sweetness.

I saw their mumble and waver over the heath
as a landscape thinking out loud

as if their tremulous thrum
were the hymn of summer pulled from sticky gorse –

a prayer that let them steer towards the taste
of a yellow star. Over my head

the day went by like a cloud,
my thoughts were a long wander.

Under the earth a pulse of slumbering bees
held me in a whirr of murmur

and drowsy meander. Drawn in
and opened out by slow thunder

I dreamt of a dark cloud in the shape of a swarm –
I dreamt a storm of honey.

When *Beowulf* Flew

through the window of Ashburnham House
the pages of his wings were alight –

words on the margins grumbled like dark bees
who flew beyond their meaning into night.

*

I've spent all summer with *Beowulf* humming in my hands
thinking of burnt words we do not have,

words we do not have when the world is a blaze
and the mind is a poisoned hive.

*

The lumbering dull gargle of a small plane
becomes this bumblebee's threnody,

he nuzzles the long grass of my unkempt lawn
turning the summer's salty light to honey.

When *Beowulf* Flew *refers to the night of October 23rd 1731, when the library of medieval manuscripts owned by Sir Robert Cotton caught fire. A contemporary account describes many of the books being saved by throwing them through the library window. The* Beowulf *Manuscript (known as Vitellius A. xv) is badly singed at the edges.*

Mrs Greenland's Hawthorn Bush

I've never slept beneath a hawthorn bush
in a warm scutch of earth on a summer's night

with a view of the river and a low yellow moon
overhearing an owl – but I think as I lay there overnight

a leaf or two might fall on my sleeping face
and maybe a pert blossom like a stringent kiss

or even a swollen haw to nestle in my ear
and whisper in the language of hawthorn.

*

That night I'd dream of petal-song,
a bright confetti of consonants,

I'd dream of a wedding in the wood –
of blood-vowel berries plangent against the snow.

Next morning I wake to hear
the mistlethrush speak his white word,

and savour the tang of hawthorn on my tongue.
Quickened with song, I walk down the hill and begin –

The title is taken from 'A Private' *by Edward Thomas:*
'At Mrs Greenland's Hawthorn Bush,' said he, / 'I slept'.

Once Upon A Pond

Winter

I once took seven steps across a pond
and felt the pang of ice

strike in seven fractures. I stood
on the other side of a small miracle,

knowing the craze of my tread
would be absorbed by melting

and made invisible. Sometimes I think
my footsteps are still in the water.

Spring

I once held a pane of pond-ice
up to my face – a loose leaf of water

clenched by winter. It stung my grasp
with a flinch of frozen breath. It spoke

a word that bit my fingers black. It was only
when I took it to the sea and kept it under

it started to shimmer and blur. By-and-by
what I held in my hands was perfectly clear.

Autumn

I once dropped a book in a pond
and saw the soaking read its pages clean.

If I swallowed a sip I tasted
the alphabet's liquorice – if I spilt

a drop I heard the murmur of verbs.
At nightfall, furls of paper rose

to the surface, and wrote in the shape
of snow-fish spoken by water.

Summer

I once lay down in a pond. I stretched
along the bend of its dried-up centre

and said to myself – now you're drowning
in air. I felt the damp pond-weed

stipple my skin, as I drowsed my spine
on a small, moist hammock. I slept

and dreamt of rain. And then I woke
and found I was filled to the brim.

66 Mill Lane

At the house where I lived as a child
my father comes out of the blue front door in his slippers.

The bonnet of our Triumph Herald's tilted forward –
he's letting the gargling radiator drink

as much as it needs from a heavy, flowered jug:
the frown on his forehead is a crease

on the surface of a stream. And singing
Younger than Springtime to herself

my mother appears at the back just as he goes in,
like Rain and Fine in a house of balanced weather.

It's another glorious day as I walk up the drive,
clunk the bonnet closed on its sprung clip

and latch the two chrome levers into place
so it won't come open by accident.

Tortoise

They gave me a stone that grew elephant feet
and a dinosaur beak. It chomped the cucumber up,

dug like a mole and kept the best secret of itself shut.
I waited a long time but it never came out.

It did not rattle when you shook it,
but I knew there was a gift inside.

To begin with I thought it was a dragon waiting to hatch.
I oiled the knobbly shell, said sorry to next-door-but-one,

wrapped it like a present and put my polished box
inside a box inside the shed. By showing me what

I could never really know, it made me a scholar.
Its silence was so heavy you needed both hands.

I loved its honeycomb lid, its stubby legs that walloped
down the lawn. I loved the blunt head and sparrow's eye.

In the end I decided it was God – and so
I penned it in a rabbit run, fed it stale lettuce

and when one spring it failed to open,
gave it a dustbin to sleep in.

The Lawnmower

My father swam the long green pool
of our summer lawn, pushing off the turn
with his feet together as the idle dolphin
dawdled its propeller until he'd completed
his poem of parallel stripes with a neat
versus at each end.

Lawnmowers measured his life:
he gathered his days in clippings.
As a child I was kept away from the growling dog
with clever teeth. He would pull the sword
from the stone again and again until
it pluttered and grumbled awake.

Now and again I would stroke it in the creosote shed.
I learnt my first curse when it would not start:
I learnt that life does not listen to what we want.
At twelve he let it drive me down the garden,
its pull and tug and we fell towards the rockery;
the dint in the big scoop. Towards the end

he bought my mother an electric.
His days were blades of grass: plenty
yes plenty but nowhere near enough.
He was making preparations for the grass
that would grow without him. All summer
we watched it flowing deep and green.

The Migraine Diary

The scratch of a spider's footstep
told him to swim upstream with curtains drawn.

Its broadcasts made him sweat:
all day they twitched and jittered in a fuzzy crackle.

He listened to the room and gathered
a black drizzle of deep thumps and gritty sparks.

A rain of days ached: scalding planets
fizzed in jagged orbits with a plum-coloured throb.

He walked in an avalanche of soot
and bitter snowflakes, searching for his own body.

When I went in to see him before bedtime
he was buried beneath himself.

The ictus of 'G' and 'Y' in his Migraine Diary
like poles to chart a footpath under snow.

Barefoot in pyjamas I follow, trying to play quietly
so I don't disturb him. As sour meteors

splinter in foggy scrawls, I head towards
the sweet blank pages of quiet light.

Measure Twice: Cut Once

They spoke a curl of wood
at each stroke. I was master
of the sky-blue dustpan.

They knew their place: the big
wooden tug up front, the neat flotilla
he'd sail across a plank.

Nothing was said. The radio sang
Until the Twelfth of Never.
He tumbled a handful on my head.

I loved the thumb-pushed spokeshave,
its furl of handlebar wings. If I twiddled
the knurled screw then woe betide.

*

I bite on the push of exhalation;
drawn back we are breathing in.

Angle my tilt and slant until
I am skimming the cream cleanly.

Your elbow a loose swing at ninety degrees
as we launch my keel on a millpond.

Rub me with candlewax stubs
as we skate to where less is more.

By keeping true I am making
your way level in this world.

Something in you is smoothed
by my touch and go.

I have made you fit for purpose
and now we are even.

*

Your edge must be kept straight,
must seat in agreement with the foot.
(A lisp to left or right and tut-tut.)

Too far and you'll suffer
the stammer of a bumpy stumble,
but nothing is shaped by silence.

Stay sharp. Hone your tongue
on the oilstone till it's keen.
If it cuts to the quick so be it.

I rub my thumb on the blade
of his voice and hear the firm
shine of his grip on things.

Four Flower Riddles

Yellow Eye

We open a yellow eye into the sun.
When our lashes blow away
we are dimpled moons or bald old men gone blind.

We point the neat arrows of our leaves
in all directions at once
because we intend to be everywhere.

Our roots go down to the first days of Earth,
we flew our seeds
before the invention of birds.

Although you do not like us
we are here to stay.
In time we shall grow over you completely.

Pink Laughter

The tide of us is always coming in.
We clamber and sprawl
and straggle a cathedral of prickles.

An open space is what we like to eat.
Our smile is lavish with spines;
our laughter a flourish of pink.

Floating over rubble and tumble-down
we dawdle by disused railways
dripping black drops of sweet rain.

When you look at our face you'll see the original rose
and also the first barbed-wire.
We're waiting until this island is no-man's-land.

Peppermint Freckles

We're printing our faces on the meadow,
peppermint freckles
smelling of fresh air and clear skies.

In a blink of years we've seen the sun grow old.
We're neat and untidy
and like to repeat ourselves repeat ourselves.

We echo the sun in our centre
with a dab of lemon;
we twinkle in sprinkled constellations.

You all look the same to us.
We'll be keeping a weather eye open
when you can't see us anymore.

Green Rain

By ditches and fallen fences we gather together
biding our time
until we have taken over the whole field.

We love whatever's broken or left behind.
We mend the skin
of earth where it's cut and hurt.

Trying to put things back to how they were
we fall like green rain.
We thrive on nothing but sunlight.

Our reach exceeds your grasp.
Leave us alone or else
our kisses will give you goosebumps.

Adder Shoelace

Long as my little finger
the adderling lay dry in the thirst of its death,
arid and crisp as a leaf, a last parched word
stuck in its throat. A dark sentence
wriggled along the spine and spoke its name;
the one remaining eye was a full-stop.

When I picked it up it was heavy
as the minute hand of a broken clock,
its moments stopped in one continual present.
And then in the shallow of my hand
as if my breath had drowned it into life
it began to curl and waver like a cellophane fish.

And when I swallowed it down there was just a scratch
as it learnt to swim. O whorl of small eel
in the well of my flesh, sing me
the riddle of the thumbprint on your head.
My bramble-thorn, my nettle-sting, my thistle,
I lie awake and listen to your venom tick.

Scarecrow

Sapling in a coat, you bear
no fruit except these drips of rain.

Little crucifixion in the field,
under your gloves the finger-buds

throb and ache. For you the hailstones
come up snowdrops in spring,

for you the hares are dancing beneath the stars.
In summer your bedraggled hat

is a dried-up riverbed, in winter the wind
blows through you, singing of ice.

Would you drop your arms if you could,
or are you the stem of an angel

blessing the stubble? Stretching to reach
the hedges and touch their green,

you wrench your welcome open.
I walk up the lane tonight

and see you lifted on tip-toe,
like someone taking a breath

before they make a swallow-dive
into the earth.

Watching the Robin

The robin who dips from our rowan tree
down to the lawn
then flits back up to spurt a scrap of song,

has found a way to open the cold afternoon
and feed on whatever he finds.
I wonder if this departure and quick return

is a robin speaking his name in the language of birds.
I wonder if maybe
I've missed what might have sustained me

or if this gazing through windows does me good.
All day I've kept coming back
to the thought of you – and how your face

has opened in me a song: can you see me
at our kitchen window,
thinking of you and smiling when he starts to sing.

Seeing the Swan

Overnight rain has left
a pool of fresh daylight in a green field –
the sky is washing a cloud

and the swan who's touching down
in a splash of shine
is a cool drop of summer for the eye to drink

as he dips his head to sip
the spilt shimmer – then lifts it again to show
the way one swan becomes 2.

Frome Valley Impromptus for Blackbird & Flute

Evesbatch Chapel

Begin with a shiver of notes –
  leaves in a churchyard wind
hap-hazards over : decide
    which ones will snag in grass
      or stick to the surface of damp
    grave slabs : this first piece
        should last as long as it takes
          to find a worm : fondly remember
        William aged six in a quiet corner

Munderfield Harold

Pull in the oars and drift –
  as overcast thins a lake
appears in cloud : watch
    for tickles of wind
      on the water's skin : long slow
    notes : a consort of foghorns
        calling to keep us from harm –
          let a floating black feather
        signal a change in the weather

Edwyn Ralph

Molehills strewn in the field
  are playing at join-the-dots –
make a shape as scattered
    and purposeful : stop for a drink
      wherever you feel like
    a sip : as the footbridge
        stretches over in ten steps
          drip a squiggle of woodnotes –
        water from a yellow beak

Halmonds Frome

Fingering splatters
  like rain in a bathtub used
as a drinking trough –
    at dusk a bedraggled shadow
      haunts the orchard : let drops
    from branches spill
        and lessen as showers
          start to ease : is that a smudge
        of sun : decide for yourself

Paunton Cross

Children on bikes freewheeling
  their laughter down a lane
reddened with haws –
    a wobble in the melody
      shows we are playing
    no-handed : the blackbird
        squinks from a hedge and can't
          seem to stop : lift up your feet
        as we splash through a red puddle

Greeve Dingle

Plinks of leaf-drip in the pool
  beneath an oak : rabbits lollop
away as we approach –
    breathe in easy wafts
      like six soft wing-beats
    from here to the hawthorn –
        roost for awhile and then
          finish after this next leaf
        has come to land

Sweeney's Songs to Eorann

Then the madman sat down upon the lintel of the hut in which Eorann was, whereupon he said: 'Do you remember, lady, the great love we gave to each other what time we were together?

i

O my watercress girl
stretched at your length in the freshet
you seem to sway and waver

in the arms of water. You've spilt a trickle of hair
a raven-dark ripple down your face.
From the pleat of a stem-clasped leaf

you open the first of your four wet petals.
Lost in the deep of your greening, I like
to pretend you're looking for me in the sky.

At our wedding you wore
the flowers of marsh and stream
wound in a circlet to swirl around your brow –

I was dipped in asphodel and butterwort,
in comfrey, codlins and cream; I was giddy
in the spill of our betrothal.

This is my watercress song,
hot in the mouth and crisp
as a kiss beneath cool sheets.

Your name is a secret well
where I sip my fill, your name
is the flower of snow.

I sing you to bring me to myself
and leave on your doorstep at daybreak
sprigs of fresh watercress.

ii

As heron I wish for the glint of your pin
my nimble skedaddler
in the shallows. I can have

my eyes on sideways, hide
in the hawthorn as a wren
to chitter you a chiding.

To be the short-eared owl
is to listen for the print of your stepfall
in the leafy night-wood.

My kestrel studies the field
where you scurry and sturt
until he has you by heart.

In your orchard my fieldfare
clatters in a smattering of apples.
As dipper I slip

beneath a drench of air,
and sip my fill in the dash
and press of your downspill.

As swallow I cleave
to the cool undershadow
of your eaves. But ah!

my clever one –
how did you become
my skylark's song?

iii

Writing to you in the sky, I haul myself
to the top of each syllable.
Caught in a feathered coat

I can't take off, my body is all misspelt –
I'm given the word *wing*
when I think of *hand*.

Whenever you see an alder remember
I loved them. Whenever you sing
remember I loved your voice.

Printing your name on the wind
in the swoop and dip of each letter
I'm lifted and held aloft.

If a feather is also a pen
then words are a form of wings
and flight-paths on paper

are birds that flutter in the mind. There is your sky
where the thought of me trembles
when remembered.

Try to keep up to the garden. Say to yourself
He's gone for a dance in the clouds.
Find a good home for the books.

And if you think on, scatter some crumbs in winter –
I'll come to our garden singing
the notes of your name.

The plight of the birdman Sweeney, that piercing allegory of mental derangement and physical displacement, will be most familiar to modern readers through his roost in Seamus Heaney's Sweeney Astray, *a rendering of* Buile Suibhne. *These poems record vestigial memories of his human love, while* Sweeney Come to Ground *finds him mourning for his lost bird-self.*

Sweeney Come to Ground

They brought with them locks and fetters to put on Suibhne, and he was entrusted to Loingseachan to take him with him for a fortnight and a month [...] and at the end of it his sense and memory came to him, likewise his own shape and guise.

I try to recall how it's done
to be a man – a splintered twig
with nothing of a song blowing through.

I say, *I've flown back to my body*
like a bird to its nest. But now
that it's over let me tell you:

my thoughts were nothing but leaves –
befuddled in a luffy bluster
I arrived wherever I was gone to.

This morning I looked for myself
in this face I find myself in, and found
a lake where leaf-minnows roost in an oak.

Forgive me and then forgive me –
for now I must learn to be sorry
for the bird I was: *sorry, sorry, sorry* –

all the song I have left. Earthed
in the shape you call me, I wonder
if sapling-feathers beneath my skull

are waiting for spring to find
a fresh unfurling. I listen
as the eagle on the hill

opens his wings to let the acorns fall.
I look at geese unleafing, at a slow
arrow of birch migrating north.

Sanicle

When his nephew was transformed into an eagle
Gwydion found his way to the secret roost

and sang three magical englyns
            with words he'd made out of flowers –
nurturing bees which sweetened him back to himself.

And so, whenever I'm cursed with stormy wings and twisted beak,
will you find where I am and sing me into my skin?

Let your song take the shape of flowers,
            star-frost blossoms of sanicle
floating to where I skulk in a staghorn oak.

Each petal a note of snow to make me sane
as we stand in a dark rain of spent plumage.

Pennyroyal

In the nests of wrens, pungent and highly aromatic,
it produces a song with greenish-yellow notes
to purify the blood and clear the air.

In the pages of John Clare's notebooks
it is there to preserve the words, and also
to keep him safe against 'the swimming in the head'.

In the shelter of an ash, caught by a sudden shower,
it's the glister in your hair as we listen
to the downpour of a wren.

Comfrey

When a cloud in the shape of a comfrey leaf
(broad at the stem and trailing to a curled tip)
drops anchor over our house,

we drowse all day under its long hull
swim in the cool lagoon of its deep shade,
and watch the blossom drizzle until we're beguiled.

We see a cup that was shattered mend itself
as each brittle splinter clings to its partner.
At night when it moors on our roof

we are nuzzled and lulled and lapped in a cat's-tongue kiss.
By morning we are one plant with two stems
and a root of twenty toes to keep us firm.

Tansy

If I left a trail of tansy –
pungent blebs of yellow calyx-stubs
in a trickle of sticky glimmers;

smutches of smouldering sulphur,
like guttering candles rank
with the phosphorous reek of a dud firework –

would you follow the spores
like dabs of spilt butter scented with pepper,
or a dribble of lemon pips;

would you swallow the salty words of tansy language,
and be led by a song
whose notes are the buttons down your blouse?

I wait at the end of yellow. When you see me
ahead in the sunlight call my name, but call my name
so softly I don't turn round.

Feverfew

Sleep with a clasp of feverfew round your wrist
and you'll see its feathery stems
rise and become a flower-cloud over the garden.

You'll walk in a slow drizzle of lemon rain
stopping whenever you want
to let the drench of petals wash you fresh.

You'll find a summery lake of spilt flowers
and bathe for as long as you like
cupping your hands to catch the tumbling blossom.

You'll let your migraine go into a thrum of deep gold
a sun-drop for bees to feed on
as you dive beneath the surface and find yourself

falling all over the garden in a warm shower
and coming to rest at last
in the yellow and green calm of waking up.

Mullein

Crush the soft petals into your ears
and wrap your feet in a swathe of yielding leaves
then walk along the air on a rope of breath
knowing the sky is a dance of blue beneath you.

Remember when making your way from cloud to cloud
to take it a step at a time. The knack to crossing over
is to see yourself there already looking back:
here you come towards your waiting self.

If anyone asks – you're training to be an angel.
And as for how it's done: recall that drunken night
you followed a white plank down the middle of the road
with never a glance at the chasm on either side.

Hyssop

If I made you a mobile out of hyssop
and hung those pungent stems in a dangle of spills

I'd know that while you lolled in a white bath
letting the bitter hyssop breathe you clean

you'd see a shoal of dawdles loop and tilt
until you felt the bathtub lighten and lift

and taking the seashell mirror for its partner
curl in a slow parabola round the house

as though to trace the arc of your unwinding
as it slips in a neat ellipse out of the window

off down the street on a waft of honey-bee-blue
and gone like a warm comet on a cruise of ease

Horehound

If I go to your house on Clegg Street
and wander through rooms demolished after the Blitz
will I find the water-butt full of Salford rain?

And if I remove the dustbin lid on the top
and drop your name like a stone through black water,
will you find your way to the surface

and develop like a portrait in a darkroom
until I can see your face your glasses your smile
and the scar on your thumb from a rose,

as you float on the brim and tell me to pay attention.
This is horehound you say, remember.
Horehound I say as you pass me a stem to hold.

Dog's Mercury

So called because
these pliable fronds are the stem
of a green thermometer –

the wood's first
thoughts on coming to itself.
Remember

the silver tears
that splashed on the bench
when you kissed

with heat a coil
of indolent solder? Those flowers
are awash

in this wood –
I step among a freshly-dripped shimmer
crushing the stalks

to release a secret blue,
as if I were melting dog's mercury
into the sky.

Evenlode

When I say Evenlode I mean
falling in love with a river
seen from a train

a river that arrives
in a gather of trickle-byes
and spill-throughs

and swells in a green swirl
and does not mind how far
before it ends

because it's there already
completed and beginning and
coming to itself by going

*

And when I say Evenlode I mean
falling in love with a wander
with the furl and curve

of learning how to unwind
in loops of slow collapse
through an open field

as a long green frond
that speaks of ease
seeps through soft ground

discovering itself
through the scrawl
of going astray

When I say Evenlode I mean
water is a fluency of touch
between two distances

like the river we make
by sleeping back to back
with the darkness warm

and softly breathing us close
while night flows past
and all the stars are minnows

as we sigh and release
until in the end we find
our way to be lost

*

And when I say Evenlode I mean
I'd be happy to drift from beginning
to end if I could

I'd follow my flow
and allow myself to be
unravelled by meanders

I'd come to my senses at last
by way of waywardness –
on the swell and lull

of a river that
goes where it will
I'd be full to the brim

When I say Evenlode I mean
a sway of silence floated
down the page

a ripple of space between
these islands of saying
where the eye

which follows their drop
through cadence
and nuance

can hear the shape
they have and also keep
because of quiet

*

And when I say Evenlode I mean
the turns that water takes
to make itself

a river that touches
the taste of each field
and keeps it fresh

until in the end it arrives
where it needs to become
because it was there already

and gone before I came
in a curl of green water
seen from a train

Oversteps Books Ltd

The Oversteps list includes books by the following poets: David Grubb, Giles Goodland, Alex Smith, Will Daunt, Patricia Bishop, Christopher Cook, Jan Farquarson, Charles Hadfield, Mandy Pannett, Doris Hulme, James Cole, Helen Kitson, Bill Headdon, Avril Bruton, Marianne Larsen, Anne Lewis-Smith, Mary Maher, Genista Lewes, Miriam Darlington, Anne Born, Glen Phillips, Rebecca Gethin, W H Petty, Melanie Penycate, Andrew Nightingale, Caroline Carver, John Stuart, Ann Segrave, Rose Cook, Jenny Hope, Christopher North, Hilary Elfick, Jennie Osborne, Elisabeth Rowe, Anne Stewart, Oz Hardwick, Angela Stoner, Terry Gifford, Michael Swan, Denise Bennett, Maggie Butt, Anthony Watts, Joan McGavin, Robert Stein, Graham High, Ross Cogan, Ann Kelley, A C Clarke, Diane Tang, Susan Taylor, R V Bailey, Alwyn Marriage, John Daniel, Rebecca Bikau, Simon Williams, Kathleen Kummer and Jean Atkin.

For details of all these books, information about Oversteps and up-to-date news, please look at our website:

www.overstepsbooks.com